MW00979544

About Couples Communcating

About
Couples
Communicating

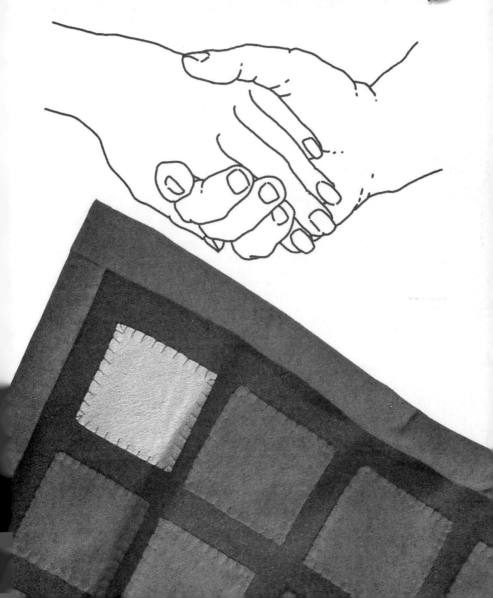

About Couples Communicating;

Melodie Dupuis

ISBN# 0-9736056-0-X
2004
About Couples Communicating
Melodie Dupuis 1948 -

Published by Harmony Publishing
4041 John's Road
Duncan, BC
V9L 6S7

First Printing 2005

Printed and bound in Canada by
Friesens
Altona, Manitoba
Canada R0G 0B0

© Copyright 2004 Mélodie Dupuis.
All rights reserved. No part of this publication may be reproduced, stored in a retrieval system, or transmitted, in any form or by any means, electronic, mechanical, photocopying, recording, or otherwise, without the written prior permission of the author.

Note for Librarians: a cataloguing record for this book that includes Dewey Decimal Classification and US Library of Congress numbers is available from the Library and Archives of Canada. The complete cataloguing record can be obtained from their online database at:
www.collectionscanada.ca/amicus/index-e.html
ISBN 1-4120-4358-1
Printed in Altona, MB, Canada

TRAFFORD

Offices in Canada, USA, Ireland, UK and Spain
This book was published on-demand in cooperation with Trafford.Publishing. On-demand publishing is a unique process and service of making a book available for retail sale to the public taking advantage of on-demand manufacturing and Internet marketing. On-demand publishing includes promotions, retail sales, manufacturing, order fulfillment, accounting and collecting royalties on behalf of the author.

Book sales for North America and international:
Trafford Publishing, 6E–2333 Government St.,
Victoria, BC V8T 4P4 CANADA
phone 250 383 6864 (toll-free 1 888 232 4444)
fax 250 383 6804; email to orders@trafford.com
Book sales in Europe:
Trafford Publishing (UK) Ltd., Enterprise House, Wistaston Road Business Centre,
Wistaston Road, Crewe, Cheshire CW2 7RP UNITED KINGDOM
phone 01270 251 396 (local rate 0845 230 9601)
facsimile 01270 254 983; orders.uk@trafford.com
Order online at:
www.trafford.com/robots/04-2166.html

10 9 8 7 6 5 4 3 2 1

ISBN 1-41204358-1

9 781412 043588

About the cover and art work:
The art work for the different reference sections was done by my daughter Zoe Dupuis and my son Toby Dupuis and the cover design was done by Ron Meyer.

Acknowledgements

I would like to take this opportunity to thank my family and friends for their support and efforts in making this self-publishing project a success. A wise friend who also edited my book, Sharon Perry, I thank with heartfelt appreciation.

I would also like to give credit to Suzanne Anderson who was extremely instrumental in helping with the use of her self-publishing reference book that I learned about in a serendipity fashion through our hairdresser, Shelly Wilson.

I would also like to thank my colleague Ron Meyer for his incredible assistance and expertise in making this self-publishing project a reality. His mentorship was priceless.

Dedication

This book is dedicated to my husband and life partner of 34 years. I asked him before I decided to write this book, what made us successful after 34 years. His response was, "Why of course Melodie, it's communication. We communicate. You know this!" His confidence was very validating.

To this day, information talking has remained the most important form of vocal communication for our species.

It [communication] acquired additional functions. One of these took the form of mood talking. Strictly speaking, this was unnecessary, because the non-verbal mood signals were not lost. We still can and do convey our emotional states by giving vent to ancient primate screams and grunts, but we augment these messages with verbal confirmations of our feelings.

Desmond Morris- The Naked Ape: A Zoologist's Study of the Human Animal

Forward

I will use the pronoun "she" rather than the polictially correct s/he. I do this not to challenge or disrespect the other half of our species, but to simplify the flow for easier reading. The priority for me in writing this book is to have the reader understand complex ideas in a friendly manner. Using only one gender pronoun, I believe will make the flow easier.

I have used authentic personal and professional examples to help explain some of the complex ideas. I have changed the professional examples to protect the confidentiality of my clients.

Thank you for reading this book and if a question needs to be asked, you may contact me through my website, www.cdfamilyquidance.com.

Contents

Introduction

The purpose of this book is to provide a tool to help couples communicate more effectively and to understand their relationship in such a way that they can grow together. You will learn about a 3-step model of self-communication, strategies using fair fighting rather than dirty fighting, and some essential skills that support a fulfilling relationship.

Relationship building is the skill of connecting with another in a fulfilling manner that allows for the meaningful sharing of thoughts, ideas, and feelings. The degree of skill employed is determined by the person with which one wishes to connect and how that connection would be meaningful.

In a more simple explanation, the success of a couple's relationship is dependent on how well she knows herself consciously and how well she can communicate that knowledge.

For example, my need to connect meaningfully with my partner, is different than my need to connect with a colleague on the job. The level of skill I employ is determined by the investment I have in making the relationship meaningful to me. What do I want out of this relationship? What am I willing to give to this relationship? These questions are asked unconsciously by self all of the time. The answers will determine just how much meaning will be brought to the relationship.

Building relationships needs to start with self. How does one go about deliberately building a relationship with self? We actually start from the time we begin formal thought. The process is osmotically learned (learned at the cellular level) by communicating our needs to our caregivers and by their responses to our requests. A person's sense of self comes from the immediate caregivers' perceptions and responses.

As I develop, I will learn about who I am through my caregivers' perceptions of me and from my immediate family members such as: parents, brothers, sisters, grandparents, aunts, uncles, family friends, etc. I will need to evaluate and question all of the different perceptions that may be coloured by their own emotional trauma, modify some, or reject some, no matter how painful the process, and explore new ones that feel right for me.

The "knowing" of self is a journey that lasts a lifetime. Even though I may have started the journey as a toddler, I will always be developing. This journey is necessary to build a meaningful and fulfilling relationship with myself and to trust myself.

The relationship I will have with myself will be very different at different developmental ages. For example, if I should sustain an emotional trauma such as the divorce of my parents at a certain developmental stage, I will need to absorb the trauma in the best way I can to accommodate my developmental stage. Then I can continue with my lifelong journey of building self-awareness. It is very important to understand and to honour the strategies that I use to absorb the trauma that I have survived. The relationship that I have with myself will determine the relationship I will have with others.

In this book I will explore the notion of honouring feelings, understanding communication dynamics, and providing strategies in building meaningful and fulfilling relationships. The key to the successful and meaningful relationship will be in how well I learn about myself and how I understand myself in relationship to the world I live in and understand. "Knowing" self is the foundation of building a rewarding relationship. It is the most demanding and challenging of life tasks and we all do it in our own unique way.

This book is a tool that may be used as a guide to help with understanding myself and at the same time this understanding helps me to share what I know about me with my partner.

Couplehood

Couplehood is a marvellous opportunity for couples to learn about themselves. Is there a reason that monogamy is so wide-spread and accepted around the world? Marital and family therapists like myself, consider the building of couplehood to be an ideal place for the final task of adult human development: self-awareness. Couplehood appears to be the perfect fit for an individual to learn more about herself, which is essential in experiencing couplehood in a rewarding fashion.

The challenge is to learn more about self so that one can share more of oneself with another. The more intimate one is with self the more intimate that one person can be with another. It is a circle, as all relationships are circles. The idea of intimacy being circular is not a new idea; all relationships are dynamic not static. There is constant change, sometimes subtle and sometimes dramatic. There are never circumstances that don't result in change. It is continuous change that helps every individual in adapting and increasing new daily self-awareness.

Learning the unconscious knowledge of self is like practising the piano. You can never stop if you want to be the best you can be. The task of learning our unconscious is a never-ending process.

My husband and I were married fifteen years before we attended a workshop for couples and learned how parallel our childhood and adolescence experiences had been. We learned that we shared many similar experiences and that we both had been designated with the same role in our families. Ironically, our cultures were very different, our languages were very different; but families are universal.

Unconsciously we each sensed a kindred spirit. We had each unconsciously chosen the same types of defense mechanisms and we were both survivors at heart. Unknowingly, we both valued the same core values. How did we know this? I really don't know but studies have shown that people recognize each other unconsciously as survivors of the same experiences, even though when they first meet, they are not consciously aware of this.

Circles within circles. Communication is a circle and it is the most important tool we have to learn about ourselves and others. Communication verbally, physiologically, or behaviourally is circular in fashion. The cycle is as follows: I send a message whether it is unconscious or conscious you receive the message and you respond whether it is unconscious or conscious. Your response elicits another response from me and so on, and so on. The more intimate the exchange, the more unconscious it becomes. Therein lies the challenge.

When the first intimate connection is made and the chemistry is felt, the scene is set for emotional intimacy. The need for your partner to understand and accept all the different roles that you bring to the relationship, then becomes important.

The roles I bring to a relationship are like the coloured shapes on a hand-made quilt. If I bring my role as mother to a relationship there are inherent boundaries with this. This interconnectedness is like the theme of shapes on a quilt making the whole from chosen parts.

An example as both a therapist and a mother, I am able to empathize better with another mother than with someone who is not comfortable with children. I will even expose my bias when a child's welfare is of concern during a separation or divorce. It is very clear to me that the child or children are unfairly caught in an emotionally painful trauma, so I am inclined to be hypersensitive to their plight. I need to be honest about this bias when working with couples, who are anticipating a separation or divorce. My need to protect the children caught in the middle cannot impede or jeopardize the therapy of the couple working on their couplehood.

The part of me that is in the role of mother is an integral part of me that is in the role of therapist. The balance needs to be fined-tuned continuously.

The perception of myself that I bring to the relationship is like the specific design of the quilt. There are many different facets of who I think I am and they all form my perception of myself through my behaviours toward others and toward myself. My core values need to have been established and that process is usually complete around the mid-twenties. This process of myself perception is explained in the chapter of the human developmental milestones covered in *Critical Periods of Human Development. (pg. 83)* A core value is something that I value and will honour no matter what occurs in my life, consciously or unconsciously.

An example that comes to mind is of a couple who were having difficulty communicating. The issue was that one spouse was most times responding to the other with what she thought her spouse wanted to hear. After a while her spouse who needed an authentic response became aware that the spouse was not authentic or genuine in her response because the same issues would come up over and over again. She didn't value authenticity while he needed it. The spouse valued her ability to accommodate rather than her ability to be authentic.

Her perception of self was developed in her childhood where to survive one had to accommodate. She unconsciously became more and more accommodating while the relationship became more and more unstable. She was eventually able to learn the difference between accommodating and authenticity but needed to honour her core value of accommodating. This was a profound part of who she perceived herself to be and she needed to value her skill at being accommodating more than she needed to be authentic in the relationship. If she were to ignore this core value she would be betraying her core self. This notion is considered an internal conflict.

My perception of my world paradigm is the lining that protects the quilt. How I perceive myself in my world allows me to take the risks that I need to take, in order to get where I want to go. My first form of defense will be to keep my sense of self safe from emotional trauma. The risks that I would be willing to take are the risks that I perceive will not overwhelm me emotionally. My perception is determined by my sense of "readiness" to absorb the emotional changes that are a consequence of emotional trauma.

The notion of "readiness" plays a critical role in taking risks. I worked with a couple for three years where one of the spouses was suffering from clinical depression. The notion of being mentally ill was too much for the spouse suffering to accept. The depressed spouse was unable to hear, let alone understand, the idea of clinical depression because the notion itself was too risky, or too emotionally overwhelming. After more than two years and some terrible emotional suffering, the spouse was finally able to hear that the suffering was a clinical depression and not psychological in origin. Only then was the depressed spouse willing to fight the clinical depression by learning everything about it and being treated for it. The information that was gained provided the safety net for the spouse to finally accept the clinical depression and it was no longer perceived to be too emotionally overwhelming. *(Types of Depression pg. 97)*

The depressed spouse's concerns about clinical depression were based on the idea of the world's perception that mental illness is seen as not acceptable. A person who suffers from mental illness is possibly dangerous, untrustworthy, and probably a financial drain on society. Having to accept the clinical depression challenged her idea of it being unacceptable to society. The reality was that she was a very capable member of society and was a valuable contributor rather than a financial drain. She unconsciously needed time to absorb the emotional trauma before she could bring it to the conscious level for acceptance and understanding.

The idea that we unconsciously need to prepare psychologically for an emotional impact is not a new idea. The concept of '*readiness'* is as real as the feelings that accompany trauma or emotional stress that have been known to cause fatal illnesses.

My perception of the way I communicate is the stuffing in the quilt. The quality of the stuffing will determine my success in getting what I believe is what I want. The levels of communication are complex, yet simple. What a paradox! Let me try to explain.

There are different types of self-communication and then there are different types of intercommunication. One type of self-communication that is extremely common is the *should* versus the *need*. The *shoulds* and the *needs*, that may reflect the conscious biases that I hold, and the unconscious biases that I hold, all need to be learned well.

So, for example, if I believed that I *should* do something, it needs to be supported by I *need* to do that something. In other words, *should* I, or do I *need* to, apologize for being late because my car broke down. I *need*, if for no other reason, to explain why I was not able to be on time, since my intent was to honour the time requested. The *should* is a form of patronization if done because it is expected rather than an honouring of the intent. So the task is to know the intent and honour it by recognizing whether, I *need* to or I *should*.

Double standards are another challenge in intimate communication. They usually reflect our unconscious biases. They are complex in nature for the simple fact that they are not easily articulated at the conscious level. The most common manifestation of a double standard is when I am criticized for something that is really a more accurate description of the criticiser than a genuine critique of my shortcomings. It is an insiduous form of negativity but extremely destructive because it is usually totally unconscious. Further discussion about double standards is found in *Types of Communication Skills and Strategies. (pg. 29).*

There are many ideas about styles of intimate communication, but I teach my clients the **3-step model of self-communication** that I have found natural and invaluable in bringing to the conscious awareness the biases and values that we hold. The following steps are a brief overview that will be explored in more detail.

Step 1.

• What am I feeling? It is important to truly understand what I am feeling. Is it anger to protect my emotional self? Is it sadness because I am disappointed? What am I feeling?

Step 2.

• Why am I feeling this way? How is it that I feel this feeling? What is my perception of the event or incident that has triggered these feelings? How are these feelings related to my sense of self? What part of me is violated, honoured, threatened, etc.?

Step 3.

• Now, what am I going to do about honouring

these feelings? The assumption is that when I make an investment in a relationship I will be continuously monitoring my feelings, thoughts, and ideas consciously. It is very important to honour my feelings, meaning that I recognize what I am feeling and I decide how to deal with the feelings in a manner that is dignified and fair to me and others.

A dramatic example for me was I was working with a client who needed to honour her feelings of violation from an experience as a young person. After working with her for some time she was able to articulate the need to mourn the loss, yet celebrate her survival. She asked if we could go to an isolated place where she could have a bonfire. So we set up a safe place for her to have her bonfire. We sat on a log and watched the fire burning until it reached a brilliant brightness then she claimed she was ready. She asked me to only witness honouring her feelings and not to participate. So, I sat on the log and witnessed her strip naked, then start to move slowly around the fire in a circle. By the time she had reached her peak, she was wailing and moving very quickly in a primitive dance of victory. When she finally ran out of energy, I bundled her up in her clothes and a blanket, then took her back to the counselling office. She was able to articulate what happened for her. She had honoured her need to let go, since the person who had victimized her was dead and she could not confront him. She felt that she honoured her anger, sadness, and strength in surviving being powerless and insignificant as a young victim, who could not protect herself.

By understanding her feelings, she was able to honour them; she found a way to let go of the loss she suffered and absorb the trauma. The feelings of violation and powerlessness will always be her legacy, but she was no longer controlled by those feelings. By understanding the depth of feelings she experienced she was able to accept the emotional trauma that she had experienced. The irony is that the more vulnerable she became the more powerful she became.

By saying we absorb the emotional pain or trauma, I speak from personal experience that is also supported by the research in the physiological reality of emotional feelings. When emotionally traumatized, the individual literally feels physical pain; the pain is registered in the same place in the brain that physical pain is registered. When someone says they were "gut punched" when referring to the shock and pain of being emotionally traumatized, it is not far from reality.

I will use an analogy of the body's physical response to emotional pain to describe how the
concept of emotional trauma is like having the
emotional part of your brain "bruised." It takes
time and considerable energy to absorb the blood
that has haemorrhaged in the bruising of tissue.
If the blood is not absorbed, it calcifies in the
muscles. The brain is referred to many times as
the main muscle in our body. So, using this analogy, if someone were emotionally traumatized
by an event in life, it would depend upon the person's ability to heal from the bruise successfully
and absorb the trauma sustained to the muscle
with minimal damage.

The absorption of the emotional trauma is then
impacted by the person's ability to absorb and
heal from the injury. The degree of emotional
trauma perceived by the individual is critical in
the absorbing process. If the individual perceives
the injury to be a major threat, it will have a totally different impact than if it were perceived
as a minor or inconvenient threat to the person's
psyche.

The individual's ability to sustain the injury is

another factor that needs to be taken into con-
sideration. Temperament and the level of self-
awareness will also play major roles in a person's
ability to absorb emotional trauma. Studies have
revealed that some children from the same dysfunctional and abusive family survive while others have little or no defense against the trauma.

The individual's current developmental stage will
also determine her ability to absorb the emotional pain. We know from the orphanages in eastern
Europe after the Iron Curtain was taken down,
that babies will literally die from the absence of
emotional attachment to another human. Babies
have died as young as 18 months of age, the victims of the terrible tragedy of orphanages trying
to respond to the horrors of social violence.

We have all heard of someone who willed herself
to die because she was emotionally distraught
about a loss in her life. Our psyches are as tangible as muscles in our cardio-vascular systems.
We are just beginning to understand the chemistry that occurs in the brain when stimulated or
battered by emotions.

Couplehood becomes an ideal theatre for both
participants to become intimate with themselves

and by doing this they are better able to be more intimate with their partner. The intimacy that comes from self-awareness creates the bonding and sense of connectedness that comes with feeling confident about "knowing" oneself. The psychological idea is known as differentiation.

Differentiation, I believe, is the foundation of success for couplehood. It is essential that the individual be as self-aware as she possibly can be, so that she can then share that self-awareness to create and maintain intimacy with the partner. I conclude in this book with a final chapter on differentiation in hopes that the idea is made clear and the understanding of the importance of this skill is realized.

Essential Skills

There are numerous relationship strategies but, according to some research, couples who consider themselves happy in their relationship also consider themselves skilled in the following areas:

- They talk *with* each other rather than talk *at* each other
- They discuss personal issues that expose vulnerabilities
- They avoid unnecessary revisiting of old topics of conflict that were thought to have been resolved

- They paraphrase each other for clarification
- They are sensitive to each other's feelings
- They are consciously aware of nonverbal communication and then are able to respond verbally
- They feel accepted by their partner because of the quality of support given during life circumstances

Talking *with* rather than talking *at*:

The notion of talking *at* someone is really a form of patronization. The message is one-sided and implies that there is no need for a response. This is a total misrepresentation of reality. The receiver may be highly insulted because she may feel that she is not important to the person sending the message. Talking *at* someone has its place but never in an intimate conversation where responses are critical.

Exploring personal values and issues:

Discussion around personal values and opinions can create a sense of vulnerability. It is important that the trust is in place for this type of discussion to occur. The trust that my partner will hear the emotion in my verbal message and understand how it is important to me, is the beginning of the working of this skill. My partner does not need to agree with me but does need to accept the importance for me. There is usually some confusion of this concept with couples. They sometimes believe that it is necessary to agree with someone in order to accept what is being said. This is not true.

A classic example, is my strong feelings about my husband's addiction to cigarettes. I understand and accept his addiction and his inability to let the addiction go, but I certainly am not in agreement with his choice. The important thing for both of us is that his addiction cannot threaten my health or my lifestyle or our commitment to our relationship. I have to accept that his addiction does impact his health and I have to accept that this is his choice.

Revisiting old issues respectfully:

The revisiting of old issues that are thought to be resolved is in itself disrespectful to both partners. The partner revisiting an old issue is not negotiating fairly but rather imposing renegotiation onto the other partner. The partner receiving the revisitation of the issue they thought was resolved is blindsided, or is feeling attacked. The revisiting may in itself be a symptom of distress in the partner who feels she needs to revisit an old issue thought to be resolved without respectful negotiation. The partner revisiting disrespectfully needs to ask why is it important to revisit? What was not resolved? What do I want from the revisitation? It is important that the interaction is consciously recognized as *dirty fighting*, and needs to become *fair fighting* instead. See discussion in *Types of Communication Skills and Strategies. (pg.43)*

Paraphrasing for clarification of feelings:

Paraphrasing and clarifying what you are hearing and understanding is crucial in intimate discussions When the emotions are overwhelming, it helps to stop the discussion or slow it down by paraphrasing back in your own words what you think you have understood. Check it out with your partner before you respond to the message. If necessary, ask your partner to paraphrase to ensure that both of you are talking about the same thing.

Paraphrasing is a means of checking out and clarifying the unconscious assumptions we make that create even more tension in the discussion. Many times, when unconscious assumptions are made, the two people in discussion are not talking together any more but talking to themselves. An indication that this has occurred is when the response that I am expecting is not forthcoming. At that time I need to slow the discussion down and begin to paraphrase for clarification. If possible, I expose my assumptions that may not be understood or accepted by my partner. If my feelings are triggered and I am feeling emotionally overwhelmed, then I need to stop and do the **3-step model of self-communication.** *(pg.33)* I may need to put the discussion on hold until I feel confident enough to be able to listen to what my partner is actually saying and respond in kind.

Sensitivity for my partner's feelings:

Being sensitive to my partner's feelings is essential in understanding the complete message. The words are usually accompanied by feelings and it is important to acknowledge both in the discussion. When both feelings and ideas are acknowledged, the partner sending the message feels validated and heard and the partner receiving the message feels confident about the discussion. Again, trust is paramount for both to express genuine feelings and then make certain that the conscious level of awareness of body language is being noted because we tend to consciously focus on the worded message.

For example when there is a mixed message, where the words don't fit the body language we may take note unconsciously or consciously. The level of intimacy shared by the couple will determine how skillfully they can read the body language. It helps for the partners to be honest about not being able to read the signals or cues and then to try to bring these signals up to a conscious awareness.

I noticed that when my husband was sometimes curt, it was not because he was annoyed but rather because he was in physical pain or terribly fatigued. It was difficult to differentiate sometimes because of the intensity of the curtness. I determined whether he was annoyed or physically uncomfortable by actually asking if what I was understanding was accurate. I learned over the years to monitor the intensity and not get hung up, or take his curtness personally. I used to be insulted at the rudeness that I perceived as targeted at me, when in fact this was not his intent at all.

Another example is that my high energy and intensity can appear to some as a signal of anger or frustration, when in fact it is really passion they are witnessing. I am a passionate and intense person. I make some people uncomfortable with these traits. I have learned painfully and over time that this is a fact of life for me. I have also learned to not take others' discomfort personally, since it is their threshold of emotion and not mine that is the issue.

The final essential skill is showing by behaviours, attitudes, and words how I accept my partner. By using these skills the acceptance becomes easy and natural. It is important to be honest with myself and then to share that honesty with my partner. It inevitably creates trust and acceptance. I need to believe that my partner's inconsideration, negativity, or criticism is not intentionally an attack on my person but a result of his need to protect his own feelings. He may not be ready for the pain that will come with his awareness of why he needed to be inconsiderate, negative, or critical.

I realize that this idea is rather difficult to understand, let alone accept. What I mean by not taking my partner's negative behaviours personally, is that I give myself some freedom to decide how I need to *respond* to the negativity. If I understand that it is about my partner's perceptions and not mine, it allows me more room to think outside the box. The more that I am able to differentiate his feelings from mine, the more I am able to *respond* genuinely and respectfully to both him and myself. I am the only one responsible for my feelings, thoughts and behaviours. This concept is straight-forward but, unfortunately, it is a challenge to learn how to take responsibility for our own *reactions* to other people's behaviours. We are not taught formally to understand this dynamic. Instead we are taught to *react* to others.

In depth discussion about this concept is found in *Types of Communication Skills and Strategies. (pg. 29)*

Types of Communication Skills

When I asked my clients and family to explain what they thought was the most valuable skill in building a relationship the answer was always "communicating." The majority of couples that I have worked with come in with the request to learn how to communicate better. They have felt they didn't really know how to talk to each other in an effective way. This chapter is the most extensive and will cover most of the areas of importance in exploring intimate communication.

To learn how to communicate intimately is not easy. I think it is important to first understand

how we communicate before we attempt to become more skilled at it. This is the most important idea discussed in this book. So I will start
from the core of communication to help you understand how simple, yet how complicated, communicating intimately is. What a mixed message
I give you! It may sound easy but it is the most
difficult idea to understand, then practise.

The most important rule in communicating important thoughts and feelings is to always speak
for yourself. The communicated message needs
to be clean. This means that the spokesperson is
only speaking for herself. The ownership extends
to how she feels. In reality no one can force you
to feel anything. If they could, they could literally control your feelings. This cannot be done.
Therefore the task is to understand how your feelings are impacted by another's behaviour, rather
than giving the person who impacted you, the
power over how you feel. When a conversation
is really important, whether with spouse, child,
family member, colleague, friend, etc., the idea
is to try to use language that really reflects what
you are thinking or feeling. The "I" statements
usually help with the clarity of the presentation.

An example is the common, "You make me so

mad." What needs to be said or understood instead is, "I am so insulted when you do this because ...." So, now I have clarified the behaviour and have come clean with my feelings about how I perceive the behaviour. The receiver of this information will need to respond to the clean message that her behaviour has triggered a strong feeling from you. It is especially important to use this language with children to help them better understand their world and the feelings that come with their world.

The common language used in discussion around feelings is to give the other person responsibility for your feelings. This practice is terribly flawed. I am the only person who can take responsibility for my feelings. Therefore, I need to demonstrate this responsibility by using language that supports my power instead of giving it away. This is a new idea for some. It may be important to practise the concept with your partner or friends. It will make a dramatic difference in the communication and will limit the misunderstandings that usually occur. You will need to be sensitive to the discomfort that some may experience when you change your style of communication during important discussions.

It is through communication that I first learn about myself. My introduction to how others perceive me will impact my sense of self. My rebellion against a perception that others may hold, that is not accepted by myself, will also impact my sense of self. My experiences in how the different roles are to be acted out will impact how I will act out roles I have chosen to accept as part of who I believe I am.

My family's perception of me as a storyteller was based on their need to deal with the trauma in our family. By labelling me the storyteller, I could not be telling the truth, therefore the trauma that we were living could not be exposed. I became an abusively honest person until I learned that I was not really the storyteller in the family but the member most likely to "spill the beans." I learned more about honesty and its complexity.

Earlier in this book I discussed briefly the **3- step model of self-communication** that leads to honouring our feelings, thoughts, and ideas. In short, it is an honouring of self. The more skilled we become in honouring our feelings, the stronger our self-confidence will become.

The most valuable quality that each brings to a

healthy fulfilling relationship, is the level of skill in communicating, which includes the ability to articulate one's feelings and thoughts, and how to listen, reflect, and then respond respectfully, honourably. Wow! I believe this is where the complications come in. It is so easy to say, but incredibly difficult to master.

I always teach the following **3-step model of self-communication** to my clients. I also needed to teach this process to myself and my family. Needless to say, we are all still working on it.

3-Step Model of Self-Communication:

Step 1. What am I really feeling?
Step 2. Why am I feeling this way?
Step 3. How do I honour these feelings?

This process is the key to communicating confidently and skillfully. It is an incredibly difficult set of skills, and we are not usually taught to communicate with self and others consciously in this way. Most times we *react* rather than *respond*.

Reacting is the filter I put between the threat as I perceive it, without understanding what and why I feel the feelings. Usually these behaviours are not guided by conscious thought. *Responding,* on the other hand, is evaluating what I feel with awareness rather than *reacting* to the message. The intent to honour how I feel about the message is the guiding force that will dictate my behaviours. *Reacting* is predominantly how we have learned to communicate our feelings. If I accept that I have learned from birth to *react* to my feelings, because it is the only way my caregiver can give me what I want, then I need to learn how to *respond* to my feelings once I have language, which is usually complete around three years of age. Ideally, once a baby starts communicating, it is time to introduce the skill of *responding* rather than *reacting* to feelings. What an ideal world this would be if this were an understood and accepted practice.

An example would be my daughter who, at three years of age, had her first mind-blowing temper tantrum. She literally threw herself down on the floor of the local grocery store and proceeded to scream that she wanted the candy I had told her she couldn't have. I was traumatized at first. I wanted to shake her until her teeth rattled, then I wanted to die of embarrassment.

Well, fortunately, I didn't shake her. (The consequence may have been the damaging of my daughter for life and I may possibly have gone to jail.) I eventually realized that being embarrassed wasn't going to get the job done. So I asked the cashier to hold my shopping-cart and I would come back to finish my shopping after my daughter had a nap. In the meantime, my daughter was really involved in her temper tantrum and I am sure she was really enjoying the experience of *reacting* to her feelings of offence at being denied what she wanted. I tried to get her attention and I wasn't successful. So I simply grabbed her by her shirt and jacket from the back and lifted her into the air. She still didn't stop. I then proceeded out the door of grocery store with this child dangling in the air, kicking and screaming. I took her home and put her to bed. By this time she had wound down and was ready to sleep off her *reaction* to her feelings. Two and a half hours later we returned to the grocery store and completed the grocery buying. The cashier complimented me on my dealing with a child out-of-control. Her experience was that many mothers were too embarrassed to deal with their out-of-control children and were not able to discipline them, losing a valuable opportunity to show a child that *reacting* in this manner was not acceptable. When she thanked me, I really felt validated and stopped beating myself up about how I had strong-armed my little daughter out of the store.

To be skilled in identifying one's feelings, one needs to be familiar with the feelings. Many of us are not in touch with our feelings because as part of surviving in our lives we have had to repress, or "stop" feeling. So the task of identifying the feelings needs to start with the vocabulary. The spectrum of feelings is joy to sadness. Anger is one of the major defence mechanisms that protects us from sadness. Anger also has a spectrum, from mild frustration to wild rage. The anger is always in proportion to the need to protect one's feelings. (If it is constantly and dramatically out of proportion the person may be suffering from a chemical imbalance or a deep-seated trauma.)

The dynamics in play when anger may be a defense to protect oneself needs to be explored. The better to explain this idea is to use some examples in which anger may be effective in protecting our emotional sense of self.

If someone ignores me when I speak to her it usually elicits a sense of resentment, which is stronger than frustration.

Using the **3-step model of self-communication** to resolve this event may look like this.

Step 1. What am I feeling?

I am feeling disrespected because the behaviour suggests that I am not important enough for her.

Step 2. Why do I feel this way?

Part of me understands that the other person is pre-occupied and another part that still impacts me daily is the legacy of the little child, who still has feelings that can be triggered about not feeling important enough for my family to accept.

Step 3. How do I honour these feelings?

The part that recognizes the rudeness needs to try to make the other person understand that the rudeness is hurtful and disrespectful. If she is unable to understand, maybe I need to become more skilled or maybe I need to let go of the notion that this person is ready to be accountable for her rudeness. Either way I need nothing from her that I cannot give myself. By acknowleding the rudeness, I also acknowledge my worth and that it is not me, but this other person's inability to understand the impact she makes on others when she is rude.

The part that is triggered by the act of ignoring me, is still tender from my feeling rejected, unaccepted, and ignored by my family of origin, and this needs to be acknowledged; it is still painful and may always carry an emotional punch. Do I need to soothe myself? Do I need to let it go? Am I ready to feel it and then let it go? Do I need to remind myself that in spite of my experiences I believe that I am worth knowing and understanding? Do I need to make a tangible effort to support my self-esteem?

Without the anger I would not need to honour my feelings of self worth. At the same time I am also protecting myself from taking on the other person's inability to honour self. By dealing with my feelings of anger I protect my tenderness about my painful experiences. This honouring is a building of self-confidence in self-awareness. The psychological idea is called empowerment.

An ineffective and dishonourable example of anger used as a defense mechanism is when another person loses her ability to rationalize her anger and is screaming abuse. The victim's response may look like this.

Step 1. What am I feeling? Am I frustrated or afraid? Am I frustrated that this person is so disrespectful to herself and me that I will not be able to resolve anything with her? If I am afraid, is it because I have experiences that say I am in danger of being emotionally and physically hurt?

Step 2. Why am I feeling these feelings? I am frustrated because it is tiring to be constantly disrespected and to keep myself emotionally safe while this verbal tirade takes place. If I am afraid, then it is because I have experiences that tell me there is possible danger to me, emotionally and physically.

Step 3. How do I honour these feelings? Whether I am frustrated or afraid, the situation warrants my either taking a time out, or the person who is out-of-control taking the time out. Nothing will be accomplished by out-of-control behaviours.

If I am only frustrated, I will need to address this issue with the other person when it is "safe" to let them know what is happening for me. I may say something like, "When you scream abuse at me and lose your control, you need to understand that I will not stay in the same room or place with you until you get yourself together. I do not want to witness your losing control because it hurts me to see you so vulnerable."

If I am afraid, then in a safe environment, preferably with a witness, I will need to tell the person who was out-of-control what was happening for me. I would say something like, "I don't feel safe in saying this to you without a witness because whether or not your intent is to physically hurt me, your verbal abuse is so emotionally hurtful that I no longer trust you or me in a situation like we have experienced."

The out-of-control behaviours are so obviously dangerous that they are more obvious to deal with in reality than the more subtle forms of emotional abuse. If I cannot deal with them because I become paralysed emotionally and/or physically, it is really important that I speak with a professional therapist to understand better what is really being triggered for me, so that I can plan how to protect myself better and learn to formulate some emotional and physical safety plans.

Building Trust with Honesty:
  Honesty about feelings with self
  Mean what I say / Say what I mean

Honesty in communication is another paradox. The more honest I am the more I may be abusive or powerful. The fine line is determined by my intent. If my intent is to feel more confident, then the honesty is powerful. If my intent is to disempower you then my intent is disrespectful and both, you and I will be disempowered.

An example, a couple that I did therapy with were having some power issues. One partner was abusing the trust of both himself and his partner. A safety plan was explored by this couple in how to deal with the next conflict they knew they would experience during the week before the next session. It was agreed that if one partner signalled the other that she was unable to continue the conflicted discussion because she was not in a safe place in her mind when her feelings were triggered, because they elicited a physical response from the interaction, then the discussion needed to stop immediately.

It was discovered that the man experienced chest pain when he was emotionally overwhelmed and the woman felt her throat tighten up. These were physiological signals that they had brought to a conscious level of awareness in order to negotiate to use them in a safety plan. The signal was for the man to make a fist and put it to his chest and say, "I need to stop." The woman would signal by clutching her throat and say, " I can't." The understanding was that the woman would write down what she perceived of the conflict and they would not discuss it until they were in session with me. Well, the man abused his power by continuing the conflict in spite of her request to stop.

First he violated himself by breaking his trust with himself and with her. This means that if he was not going to honour the negotiated safety agreement, then he believed consciously or unconsciously that she wouldn't honour it either.

The second violation was by choosing to break the trust with himself, he also broke trust with his partner, whom he knew was already traumatized by her inability to trust him and herself. When she continued with the conflict she supported his violation of the safety agreement and engaged with him in breaking the trust that they were both trying to re-establish. In the end, the building of trust was violated by both.

When he broke the trust, she needed to honour her feelings. By honouring her feelings she would repeat, as many times as necessary, "I can't," and keep eye contact throughout the exchange. She would repeat the message until either he acknowledge it or walked away. By one of them honouring their feelings, the tone and the intent would have changed immediately. He would have understood clearly that it was more important for her to honour her feelings than to win a no-win power struggle with him. More in depth discussion on power struggles in the chapter of *Power Struggles. (pg.*73)

Dirty fighting is when communication is intentionally disrespectful to protect one's self-esteem. Unfortunately the dynamics involved are counterproductive and in actuality there is a loss of self-esteem for both parties who engage in *dirty fighting* because the need to overpower is more important than keeping one's dignity. The need to overpower stems from the fear of being overpowered. To engage in *dirty fighting* is **always** a no-win situation.

I will try to explore *dirty fighting* and *fair fighting*. It is important to understand that fighting is a necessary and natural part of building a relationship. The idea that, "I want you to believe that what I think is important, is also important to you." is the beginning of a legitimate *fair fight*. All communication is sending messages for a reason. Some messages are perceived as very important and the sender may need the receiver to think or feel the same way she does.

Dirty Fighting versus Fair Fighting:

Some examples of *dirty fighting* that are more subtle than yelling, screaming, and ugly name-calling are as follows:

"You make me feel stupid." The dynamic is as

follows:

> The person who makes this statement is really saying, "I feel stupid because I believe or think that you have judged me as stupid." The *dirty fighting* is the name calling. The person who has said "You make me feel stupid." is accusing the other of name-calling, whether she has or not.

> The dignified statement would be more like this. "I believe that you think that I don't understand what you are saying and I need to know why you think that I don't understand." The dynamics are more clear, concise, and assertive. The person saying this, is not speaking for anybody but herself. The person is being very honest about what she is really thinking and expecting.

> There are no hidden assumptions to muddy the waters. The hidden assumption is that the person, who accuses the other person of calling her stupid, is making a disrespectful assumption. She needs to provide the evidence that supports this belief; she thinks/believes that the other

person actually thinks she is stupid. What does being stupid mean to each participant? Does stupid mean that one of the participants is actually manipulating the other and therefore she has perceived she has no power in the interaction because of the manipulation?

One person confronts another with a behaviour that implies some form of judgement of that person as being unacceptable. Exaggerating for example implies that the person using it is trying to manipulate the other person's perception. When it becomes an accusation it has now become an unfair judgement of that person. The response, to the accusation such as, "Well, don't you exaggerate?" A rhetorical question that implies, "You are no better than me." This statement sets up a competition. It also distracts from the main idea.

A more dignified response would be, "You think/believe that I have exaggerated the truth so that it no longer looks like the truth?"

The accusation of manipulating the truth, in this case, is never addressed when responded to competitively. It is important that the accusation be dealt with so that the real issue is explored. The real issue was the offence taken because an exaggeration was used to manipulate the receiver's perception of an event/idea. Why was it important for the person to exaggerate?

Another example of *dirty fighting* that usually destroys relationships is the use of sarcasm. Using sarcasm in an intimate communication struggle between partners is always going to impact negatively. This form of communication is designed to belittle and disrespect under the guise of humour. It is a cheap way of abusing power by appearing to be superior.

Unfortunately the user of sarcasm loses dignity and trust instead of protecting her self-esteem. The victim of the sarcasm loses dignity if she responds to it and the trust is again lost. It usually is a vicious cycle that once started is very difficult to break.

Making assumptions without clarifying the assumption with the other person is tricky. It is natural and common to make assumptions about what you think the person is really saying. Unfortunately, too many times the assumption is not correct because it is based on the judgemental person's emotional needs which have not been articulated, rather than on the person who is being judged.

The rule of thumb is to clarify with the person whether the assumption that is being made is accurate. The difficult part is that sometimes the realization that an assumption has been made is not understood.

Without clarification, a vicious cycle of misunderstanding can start. The trick is to stop the discussion once an assumption is recognized. Deal with it before continuing the discussion.

I worked with a couple who were having a difficult time with this form of vicious cycle. One partner's emotional anger was driven by an underlying personal issue. This partner was unable to absorb the emotional trauma of the underlying issue and therefore was in a perpetual state of anger. This anger coloured the lens through which she interpreted events. It became abusive because a simple act was predictably going to be seen as offensive or purposefully disrespectful, even when there was no intention of disrespect. It exhausted all participants to constantly field the anger and the intensity of the anger. This partner was not able to articulate the source of the anger, but instead created a world where everything provided fodder for the anger.

The anger is a self-defense mechanism to protect a person's psyche from emotional pain that can be overwhelming. The anger that this partner was experiencing had a deep-rooted source that could have been totally overwhelming if brought to the conscious level of thinking. The naming of the source was so terrifying that the anger needed to protect the threat of being emotionally overwhelmed was fierce.

The *readiness* factor that I believe is critical in any emotional development was in play. This partner was not ready to deal with the pain that would be articulated if the source was brought to the conscious level and therefore, until this partner's psyche could handle the emotional pain, anger was the only tool this partner perceived she had to keep the pain at bay.

I was unsuccessful in teaching more strategies to this partner and the fragility of the anger acted like a boomerang. The more the anger was used to protect her self-esteem, the more fragile the situation became between her and her partner.

Stonewalling, or refusing to respond to another's need for understanding, is the most detrimental of all the different forms of *dirty fighting*. When one partner refuses to engage in a meaningful fight about the need to be understood, the communication is totally disrespectful. The message given by not participating is that the person needing to be understood is not important. It is a very strong message and extremely hurtful. There is an unconscious assumption that there is no trust and no hopes of building trust. It is understood that my intent is to engage in a power struggle rather than resolve any issue. The power struggle is more important than honouring my feelings. It is a deadly form of distracting the communication from the real issue because the intent is to destroy the interaction and the trust in the process.

Stonewalling is different than the third step in self-communication. If I feel overwhelmed I need to say to my partner that I can't continue this fight. I am unable to think clearly because my feelings are choking me. I let my partner know that I am vulnerable and that I am doing my best to look after myself.

Stonewalling has a totally different tone and intent. The intent with stonewalling is to be very disrespectful and for the person victimized by this form of *dirty fighting* there is no response available except to disengage. This disengagement is a death-blow to a relationship. The tone is meant to punish, not protect, my sense of self. It is a conscious act, not a strategy in self-defense.

Double Standards, as mentioned earlier, are usually unconscious biases. The classic is, "I can lose my temper; you cannot." The most difficult task is to articulate this double standard at a conscious level. Once this occurs, then the exploration of the why it is in place will reveal the part of self that needed protection. It can be a simple learned double standard or it can be an extremely complex mechanism that is used to protect the core of self. Unfortunately, double standards are incredibly detrimental to relationships because they are unfair to both the holder and the judged. This unconscious communication has deep roots that need to be articulated. It is a difficult exploration for everyone because it usually challenges the holder's belief system of her core self.

Recognizing Boundaries:

What is an emotional boundary? It is like a person's physical space. Everyone has a unique emotional boundary and there is some common understanding of the different boundaries. Emotional boundaries are subtle and unique to each individual. When a boundary has been disrespected the person on the receiving end needs to acknowledge the discomfort experienced and use clear language to explain what happened emotionally for her. The person who was perceived as disrespectful may not have been intentionally disrespectful.

Emotional boundaries are distinctive to each social situation. A professional boundary and a personal boundary can be clear, yet are many times
unconsciously disrespected.

An example is emotional touching in a professional situation. If the professional is not skilled
in emotional touching she is vulnerable to violating the boundary between personal and professional. When I have had a very intense and
emotional session with clients, I have had clients
ask for a hug. The hug is given freely. I allow
them to embrace my energy because I am receiving their energy and holding it rather than taking
their energy in the hug.

If this concept is a little foreign, try and experi-
ment. Ask your partner for some time and pa-
tience. Then try to hug with different intents. You
will find that the focus changes. If I need a hug
from someone, what I really need is a physical
and emotional giving from her and I may want
to reciprocate. If I want a sexual hug, the energy
is different and there is less of the emotional and
more of the physical energy I will receive and
give. The physical touching may be exactly the
same but the intent and therefore, the energy is
felt differently. Try hugging until you are un-

comfortable. Time this and you will know your emotional and physical threshold for giving of your energy. When you become more skilled in hugging you will learn the subtle body changes that are reflected by the feelings that are being experienced.

If you monitor your hugging you will also notice that the hugs from different people will also reflect the energy given. A hug to a child is very different from an adult because the child is totally innocent and her energy is all about taking and not really giving. A child is not developmentally ready to give her energy but is still in the stage where she needs to take the energy.

Physical touch is powerful. Whether we are conscious or not of the intent for the touching, we respond with feelings. Intent is always discernable but the understanding may be difficult to bring to the conscious level. As we develop socially and intellectually we focus more on verbal messages rather than on physical messages. It appears to be a natural result of learning language.

I believe that we are not usually taught to understand that every emotional response is felt in the body. Biologically, chemicals are released in the brain and body to allow us to experience the emotional response. Therefore, the neurological development that occurs before the age of 12 prepares us for the spectrum of emotional responses that we are able to feel.

The physical and emotional connection:

Earlier, I mentioned physical responses to emotional feelings. When I work with couples I will always ask them to identify where on their bodies they feel the emotional stress. This physiological response is important to recognize because it gives the person a chance to understand that she is emotionally engaged at a cellular level. The physical and emotional connection need to be acknowledged. This physiological response is usually the first indication that the person is overwhelmed emotionally and the body is letting the person know.

Everyone is different. I feel like my sternum has been punched when I am emotionally traumatized. I have had so many different responses from my clients that I think it is important for you, the reader, to try to identify your own. Where do you feel the tension on your body when you are involved in an emotional discussion? It is really important to understand this connection.

I use the term *"hooked"* for this development. When I am *hooked* it is because I am feeling the physical response to my overwhelming feelings. This overwhelming of my feelings critically impacts my thinking and puts me at risk to do or say something hurtful to myself or partner.

Once you can identify this physical response, you will know that this is your emotional threshold. To continue in a discussion when this physiological response has occurred is putting yourself at great risk for emotional pain. This response is a strong indicator that you are emotionally overwhelmed and need a time out to come down from your body's adrenaline response and to think through what happened. Only when you are clear about what you were feeling, why you were feeling what you felt, and know what you are going to do to honour your feelings, can you safely return to the discussion and be productive.

When you have understood this concept and know how to honour your feelings then you are ready to use a conflict/resolution model to resolve the issue that was being discussed.

The conflict/resolution model that I use is a 4 step model. I will discuss the steps in detail and provide some strategies.

Step 1. Identify the problem

Step 2. Brainstorm an acceptable solution

Step 3. Create an action plan to resolve the problem

Step 4. Evaluate after action plan has been done

Identifying the problem may be the hardest step. Here are some tools to help with the sussing of the problem.

Reflective listening: means that you reflect back in your own words what you thought your partner has said. She clarifies and accepts that you have the idea.

Paraphrase: means that you use your own words to try to put into words what you think your partner is trying to say. This is different from reflective listening. Reflective listening is just a small piece of the information, an idea, no more, while paraphrasing is giving back a bigger chunk of information including the feelings that you think you are hearing.

Open-ended questioning: means that you avoid at all costs the question "why?" The reason being that "why" puts the listener on the defensive automatically. It is too big. So, when you want to know why, try using something else to solicit the understanding you need. It forces you to break down the problem into smaller pieces of information, which makes it easier to understand and clarify in identifying the actual problem.

Dignity is a must. If you should get emotionally *"hooked,"* meaning that you're experiencing a physiological response to your feelings, you will need to stop until you have control of your thinking again.

Allow each person to complete what she needs to say, even when you think you know what she is going to say. It is important sometimes, to just be able to say it. She is honouring her feelings. By hearing her out you set a tone of trust.

Learn the body language of your partner and respond with respect. When you think she has been "*hooked*" and it appears that she doesn't realize it, let her know what you are seeing and ask her if she is "*hooked.*"

To be "*hooked*" means a signal to **always** stop the discussion until you are both ready to continue. A personal example was eventually allowing my husband three months to work through a painful issue for him so that we could discuss the impact on our relationship. Every time we would try to discuss this painful issue he would get "*hooked*" and needed time to be ready to understand his feelings before he could share them with me. It was terribly frustrating. I was chomping at the bit, but he needed the time and I needed to honour that.

Evaluating the way a solution was experienced is not always done in the conflict/resolution process. It really is important to have a discussion around how it worked. What worked? What didn't work? The evaluation is the most important tool in becoming truly skilled in conflict/resolution. This stage is where the actual learning is solidified. Time for the evaluation discussion needs to be incorporated into the conflict/resolution.

Many times when this process is attempted, the

evalution process exposes how the identification of the problem was not accurate or as clear as the couple thought. Most problems are complex and need to be broken down into smaller issues or conflicts.

In the next chapter of *Strategies for Emotional Survival (pg.61)* you will be able to learn more about how to understand the whole picture of the impact of resolving issues for you and your partner. Emotional strategies need to be understood and respected since they provide us with protection from being emotionally overwhelmed.

Strategies for Emotional Survival

There is always a perceived benefit for our choice of defense mechansim. The task is to understand what the benefit is. Every behaviour has a rationale that is unique to each individual. The rationale allows the individual to experience a sense of emotional safety by choosing the defense mechanism to protect her emotional safety.

Some of the strategies used to deal emotionally with our feelings are unconsciously learned. Most strategies that we use are a direct *reaction* to the need to absorb a perceived emotional trauma. Emotional strategies are the defense mechanisms that I discussed in the previous chapter. I've tried to identify some common strategies so that I can explain the dynamics.

Disassociation:

This type of defense mechanism is usually unconscious and can be used dramatically or subtly. Dramatically, would be when the self is literally emotionally not present in a physical sense.

A client with whom I have worked had been regularly sexually abused as a toddler by her grandfather. She disassociated during the experience, meaning that she literally was not emotionally present during the sexual abuse. The abuse usually took place in the bathtub. As an adult she was unable to take baths because she felt extremely vulnerable sitting in the bath rather than having a shower, where she was able to move around. The ease of getting in and out of the shower gave her a sense of safety. When she finally was able to absorb the trauma of her experience of sexual abuse, she needed to honour those feelings of vulnerability and safety. She is able to have a bath now, but still experiences the strong sense of vulnerability. She honours her sense of vulnerability and celebrates the strength of accepting this vulnerability without it impacting her lifestyle negatively. When she takes a shower or bath she has set up a simple routine of having a transparent shower curtain and a can of hair spray close at hand. She needs to play out this routine to honour her feelings of vulnerability. If she never learns to be comfortable in a shower or bath and always feels vulnerable in the bathroom, it is an unfortunate legacy from her grandfather. She has mastered the fear and that is what is the most important part of the "knowing" about herself.

This "knowing" of her emotional self awareness, gives her power. The vulnerability has become now a strength because she is aware of what she is feeling, why she is feeling the emotion, and she is now honouring the feeling.

A subtle disassociation example would be a middle-aged man I worked with who had experienced emotional trauma from his step-mother. In his adult relationship with his spouse he was unable to stay focused on the conversation if his spouse became agitated about his forgetting an errand or task for which he was responsible.

When he realized that his disassociation was his way of avoiding the painful experience of having to relive the emotional trauma, he began to find a creative way for his spouse to help him stay focused. They invented a signal that only they knew and then, when the emotion was triggered, both understood that he needed to take a deep breath and let her know when he was able to deal with taking responsibility for his forgetfulness. The forgetfulness and the behaviours diminished noticeably after they both started to work on his disassociating.

These examples are classic of how mis-communication can take place. The spouse felt disrespected and misused, while the man felt he was being victimized again. It created a no-win situation. By learning how he had used a strategy as a child to survive emotionally, he was able to honour this strategy by using it in a more balanced and effective manner. His spouse's honouring his experience was necessary to break the vicious cycle that they had created and in the process, they built profound trust.

Denial of feelings:

The strategy of denial is psychologically an essential component of adjusting to trauma. When a death or emotional shock occurs, the psyche needs time to prepare for the onslaught of feelings that accompany the emotional trauma. The first phase is denial. The second phase is anger, and the third is acceptance. These three phases may overlap, but usually one of the phases is dominant. All three defense mechanisms are necessary to absorb emotional trauma.

An example that comes to mind of the mother who responds heroically to her child who was involved in a life-threatening experience. The mother of this child literally lifted a 1700 pound vehicle to free her child from beneath the vehicle that had rolled on top of him. She later had to be hospitalized for torn muscles and tissue, but at the time of the incident the brain blocked out the pain because her child's safety overwhelmed her emotional senses. Her ability to totally deny her physical feelings was superhuman because her emotional trauma was over-riding everything else.

Another less dramatic example is that when a person learns of an unexpected death, the person often *reacts* with a denial. The death could not have happened, or no, it is not possible. The brain needs time to adjust to the emotional trauma of accepting the loss. Then the person may experience anger; it is necessary to honour the fact that the death was not negotiated, that the death was unfair, and that the emotional trauma from the loss is overwhelming. The anger is a powerful defense mechanism to allow time for the brain to prepare for acceptance. The final phase of absorbing trauma is the acceptance of the impact of all the changes that occur from trauma. Each individual is different and each individual will deal with the three phases uniquely. The overlapping of the three phases will appear in the parts that the person has intellectually conceptualized.

The ability to absorb the emotional trauma is impacted by my sense of self which plays a major role in how I will adjust to change. My self awareness will be the foundation of my adjustment to the change. Each traumatic change will be different and will have a different flow through the three phases of absorbing trauma.

For example, a client I worked with had been laid off from his job because of government cutbacks. It was not foreseeable and therefore he was unprepared for the trauma of the loss of his job. He needed to stay in denial about the unfairness for a short period of time, but he needed to experience the anger phase longer, even while he was denying that the cutback was a logical financial reaction to a government that values services differently than he did. The anger was needed to fuel the acceptance of getting on with his search for a new job, that may have been an improvement, rather than a punitive change for him. The acceptance of losing his employment took him a longer period of time to absorb. He was able to make this change a positive one as we worked through accepting the anger that was necessary to honour the unfairness of the cut-backs. He is still feeling the righteous anger of losing his job to a whim of government, but he is able to absorb the loss and it no longer overwhelms his energy. His experience in the three phases of absorbing a change or loss, was unique to his ability to intellectualize his feelings and accommodate his perception of the world with those feelings. His biggest challenge was to honour his anger. He was overwhelmed by the unfairness and needed time to adjust, intellectualize, and absorb the emotional blow he had received when told of his unemployment. The perception of each emotional trauma will dictate the flow of the three phases we experience to absorb a perceived loss.

Lying:

Lying is a social. To lie to oneself is another form of denial. To know and tell the truth is too painful and therefore, one needs to make it a nontruth. It creates a type of self-victimization. Not being able to tell the truth indicates an inability to absorb the emotional trauma underlying the necessity of lying to oneself.

When a person uses self pity to avoid the pain of feeling rejected or unacceptable, the person is truly disempowering herself. What is the benefit of being disempowered? Is it to avoid responsibility for one's behaviour? Is it to provide a false sense of sadness to keep people from exposing the emotional pain that one may perceive as too painful? This defence mechanism is again a form of self-victimization.

Anger is the most obvious defense mechanism because it is so tangible. This self defense mechanism is a powerful defense from overwhelming emotional pain. An angry person is emotionally vulnerable. Anger can be destructive or it can be effective enough to save a life. Anger that is not understood and is used out of balance can create serious harm to the angry person and her victims. On the other hand, anger used to protect self can be very effective if used skillfully.

An example is an experience I had when I was 30 years old. I was working with troubled youth at the time and I apparently looked younger than my 30 years. One of my charges, an eighteen year old male, tried to make a sexual pass that was totally inappropriate and disrespectful. I called him on it and he became very angry because he felt humiliated in front of his peers. Unfortunately, he was trained in violence by his family and without thinking, tried to physically assault me. I used anger to deal with him. I had been taking martial arts for about two years by then. So I immobilized him by pushing him up against the blackboard and then put him in a tight hold. I said quietly, but with conviction, that we both needed to figure out what we were going to do now. He realized his predicament and that some of his peers were ready to defend me if he should break free from my hold. We were able to negotiate, and in the end this young man became one of my best leaders in his peer group. The young man realized that I was angered by his violation of me, but that I was not paralyzed by his assault. My anger became more powerful than his because I was able to use my anger to protect myself.

Another strategy commonly used is the need to constantly criticize others. She is in reality trying very hard to deny her sense of inadequacy. The person who is receiving the criticism is occupied in defending herself and will not usually look to the person who is doing the criticizing. If the criticized person were to acknowledge the criticism by paraphrasing it back to the critical person, the strategy of constantly criticising others is no longer effective. By acknowledging the criticism, it allows the person who was on the receiving end to not take the criticism personally. When the critical person realizes that the person she is criticising is no longer emotionally invested, the strategy is no longer useful in supporting the denial of inadequacy.

For example, when I was working on an assignment for my undergraduate degree, one of my peers criticized my high energy level. Instead of taking it personally, I paraphrased back to her what I believed she was really saying to me, "You are really not comfortable with my high energy are you?" She was taken by surprise and had to think before she responded. It was her perceived inability to effectively multi-task and not my high energy that was the real concern. She had judged herself to be less than she really was by trying to compete with my inherited high energy. She beat herself up emotionally because she felt that she *should* be as successful as I was in multi-tasking.

The strategies used to protect oneself from being overwhelmed emotionally can be truly creative. The need for self defense from emotinal pain needs to be honoured. If the strategy victimizes self or others, and impacts a person's or persons' physical or emotional safety, this warrants professional help. Addictions are considered the most detrimental strategies of self-victimization.

Addictions:

The self-victimization of addictions is identified by the intensity of the relationship the person has with the activity that she is addicted to. If the person's first relationship is with the activity and not with self, you know that she is addicted.

A painful personal experience that was an invaluable learning experience was my effort to sustain an intimate relationship with a family friend who used alcohol to self-medicate her inability to absorb the emotional trauma of her childhood. Her addiction was a strong barrier to our ability to communicate meaningfully and respectfully. My need to acknowledge that her relationship with the alcohol was more important than her physical and emotional safety was a painful realization.

As I mentioned earlier, no one can have a meaningful relationship with an addicted person because all her energy goes to the activity. The activity is a strategy that allows the user some relief from the emotional pain that she believes can destroy her emotionally. It is the most vicious of self-victimization cycles. Professional treatment is always needed.

Strategies that we use to protect our sense of emotional safety can be incredibly innovative. Some are out of balance and just need to be fine tuned while others need to be replaced. The important task is to understand that a strategy is actually at work in the interaction with self and/or others. Without this awareness the understanding of self cannot begin.

Power Struggles

What is a power struggle? What is the abuse of power? What is empowerment?

I will explain and discuss these three questions to help with understanding the connection between the perception of self and the perception of power that the self has.

Every communication, whether it is through body language or words, is a two-way interaction. **Always.** The communication can be conscious or unconscious. It can be overt or covert. The intent of the communication can be subtle or assertive; even if there appears to be no response, there is in fact a response. All of it has meaning.

We all respond to the meaning consciously and/ or unconsciously.

A power struggle can occur in all of the ways explained. If one person communicating her needs overpowers another, then it becomes a power struggle. I will give examples for the different explanations of communicating that I will explore.

The obvious is the physical overpowering when someone becomes intentionally dominant. An example is when I lost my cool with my husband because his teasing got to be more than I was able to handle at the time. I punched him in the upper arm towards the shoulder. My husband's first language is French and he has learned the term "child abuse" for physically abusive behaviours. This in itself is a long story, but not for the telling now. So, when I punched him, he exclaimed indignantly in his unique English that I was "child abusing" him. I was trying to overpower him in my struggle to make him understand that I could no longer handle the teasing.

When my husband identified the violation that was an attempt to overpower, he diffused the power struggle. I was given the choice of either accepting my behaviour as a violation and therefore apologizing, or play the power game alone.

Violence is always a poor form of communication and it can put a person in jail if taken to extremes. But the bottom line was that I had overstepped an emotional boundary and had violated my husband physically and emotionally.

A more subtle form of physical overpowering is the violating of a person's physical space. Moving into someone's personal space intentionally is seen as an attempt to overpower someone. There does not need to be any verbal language used, just the physical behaviour. This is an intentional violation of a social rule or our cultural mores.

Another example of a subtle form of a power struggle taking place is the eye contact that our North American society demands when we speak to each other, if not received the communicator is offended. If there is no eye contact, the person trying to communicate may feel that she is not important enough to warrant the socially accepted eye contact expected.

Another form of a power struggle employed

through language is blatant name calling. The unfairly judging of another is always a violation. In our North American culture it is more than common to name call. We forget just how damaging that can be to others. The intent in using name calling in a power struggle is to judge another less than who she is. In the process the abuser experiences a sense of superiority for a short period of time. Again, the power balance is out of whack. The sense of superiority is short-lived, leaving the abuser feeling more inferior than ever because she cannot sustain the feelings of superiority.

I am sure everyone has had her "buttons pushed," and has *reacted* to the emotion felt rather than understood the impact the feelings have had on her. Buttons that can be pushed are emotional issues that still have some sting to them. Sometimes they are consciously known and sometimes they are not. When the emotional issue is not at the conscious awareness, the chances of *reacting* to the emotional threat rather than *responding*, are very great.

Reacting is to respond with behaviour that is not really thought out and is usually a reflection of the degree of emotional pain that is perceived. The *reaction* is directly related to the fear of feeling emotional pain, and consequently, it dictates the behaviour. By *responding* to the button pushed, a person recognizes the emotional issue, why it needs to be protected, and then determines the best way to deal with keeping herself emotionally safe.

I mentioned earlier the idea of *reacting versus responding* in *Types of Communication Skills and Strategies. (pg.29)* If I am not aware of my emotional buttons I am at risk of *reacting* rather than *responding* to my feelings. Power struggles are infamous for exploiting emotional 'buttons."

Another form of engaging in a power struggle is to patronize the person to whom I am speaking. I speak to them in such a way as to negate their existance. I am really talking *at* them and not *with* them.

An example is being lectured for something that we both know I understand already. Another example is to have the person I am talking to treat me as if what I am saying is not valuable. Also in some *dirty fighting*, one partner will not let the other have a say, and when she finally allows the other to talk she doesn't listen to what is being said. The end result is the patronizing of the receiver who is given the message that she is not important enough to have an understanding, or an opinion worth listening to. When I have experienced patronization by someone, I have felt as though they have totally negated my person. I don't exist for them!

One of the most powerful and dangerous types of power struggles is the use of *lying* with the intention to influence the receiver and put her in jeopardy. If she believes the lie, she becomes vulnerable, which is the intent of this type of lying. It not only destroys trust, but leaves the liar feeling vulnerable because she knows she is on shaky ground. The fear of getting caught is always stressful. It is a no-win situation for both liar and victim. When a person is unable to acknowledge that she has lied and it is blatant that the liar believes the lies, there is an underlying personal issue going on. I would recommend that the couple seek professional help in working through the hurtful and intentional lying.

Non-engaging in a power struggle:

As I mentioned before, communication is always a circle. A power struggle is occurring when it is more important for me to overpower your sense of self than it is for me to honour my sense of self. My need to protect my sense of power is stronger than my need to honour my sense of self and my feelings. The task is to:

- Recognize the power issue
- Not respond but instead honour feelings
- Learn to *respond* instead of *react*

These concepts are again very difficult skills and parallel the **3-step self-communicaiton model**. We are not taught formally about these concepts and most of us learn from trial and error or from the strong need to survive emotionally. Most times a power struggle will elicit a physical response. Stop and think for a minute. Where on your body do you feel the tension when you are emotionally upset? When you know where on your body you feel the tension, you will know this physical response is an indication of engaging in a power struggle because you are emotionally overwhelmed. I use the term "*hooked*," which means that I am unconsciously *hooked* into playing out the power struggle because I can no longer understand the issue that is in play. I am sure you will understand that this is again a no-win situation.

The only solution to dealing with a power struggle is to not engage and to honour your own feelings. So, when you have realized that you are now engaged in a power struggle, you need to go through the **3-step model of self-communication** and honour your feelings.

I was working with a high-functioning autistic youth. His behaviour was potentially dangerous to himself and his peers. I needed to stop him because I felt unsafe because his behaviour was unpredicatable. I used my body, without touching him, to separate him from his peers. I continued eye-contact, which made him very uncomfortable, and repeated my statement that he needed time out until he finally acknowledged me. After many sessions like this he began to learn that I would always honour my need to respond to his unsafe behaviour, I would not ignore it, ever. Later he only made a half-hearted attempt to engage me in power struggles because he realized that I would honour my feelings of feeling unsafe. It had become a safety net for him.

I have found that if I know what the issue is for me in the power struggle that is presented, then I know how to honour my feelings. By honouring my feelings, I bypass the power struggle and deal with the real issue at hand. If I don't know what the issue is for me then I need to take a time-out to figure it out. By taking the time-out I once again by-pass the power struggle. The message always given is that my feelings are more important than this power struggle you need to engage in.

Most times a power struggle occurs because of misunderstood perceptions. It is tricky, but necessary, to learn if there is a misunderstanding about what my partner perceives. If I don't learn this, it usually leads to making disrespectful assumptions.

If I think that my partner is making an assumption that is disrespectful or wrong, I am honour-bound to clarify it with him immediately. The discussion needs to stop and the clarification needs to happen before the discussion can continue. Both partners need to know that they understand the same thing in order to continue a meaningful and rewarding discussion, or *fair fight*.

Usually a time-out is always necessary when *dirty fighting* begins. The physical separation can be as easy as leaving the immediate premises and finding a safe place to work through the emotional stress of being in conflict. Other times it may be more difficult. No matter what the time-out is, it is necessary to stop the *dirty fighting* immediately.

I have been married over 34 years and we both still make disrespectful assumptions of each other. I have issues that will always be a part of who I am because I have lived what I have lived. If I am not careful, they get in the way of how I perceive what is happening. If anything, the irony is that the longer we know each other the greater the risk of making the wrong assumption. The awareness from intimate relationships is so complex and so great that it becomes too easy to make the wrong assumption because we have this arrogance about "knowing" the other so well that we take liberties in judgement that may get us into trouble.

Critical Periods of Human Development

In this chapter I will explore and discuss how the critical periods of human development impact, influence, and create our understanding of self and others. First I need to take the time to identify each critical period or window of human development and explain its significance.

Attachment:

Emotional attachment is a critical developmental issue because it supports the notion that people can die from emotional pain. Babies in orphanages after horrific wars have died because they were not able to experience enough emotional contact. The human brain literally needs to be emotionally stimulated to grow. If there is not enough physical touching, eye contact, and emotional communication between the infant and its caregiver, the baby will literally lose its life. The significance is, that if an infant never begins the process of attachment, all human attachment is impossible; there will be no brain cell development to support the emotional development.

Language acquisition:

By the time a toddler has reached three years of age their ability to hear all vowels has stopped developing naturally. This is the universal age at which a child can learn multiple languages without any accents. Language is defined as ideas that contain a subject, an action, and an object or the person/thing having the action done to it. The communicating at this level is considered still primitive, but the toddler is able to express ideas, whether it is through sign language or verbal words. The emotional attachment includes intimate family members at this stage.

Imagination is critical in a child reaching full in-

tellectual potential and is now visible in the behaviour of a toddler. The child needs to use her
imagination without formal guidance or censure,
to stimulate the neurological development needed for later stages of development.

Developing a Social Conscious:

A child needs to learn how to empathize before
the age of eight. She needs to understand and experience how others feel because it helps her to
know what she is feeling. If she has not been
taught empathy by this age her ability to learn
empathy is almost non-existent after ages 8-10.
This socialization process is critical in learning
how to communicate one's feelings and ideas.
The emotional attachment now will begin to include adults and peers outside the family unit.

At the age of 12 the brain has completed all the
primitive pathways and will no longer form new
ones, but will now complete the development of
those pathways. This is because the brain needs
to complete the social, emotional, sexual, and
physiological systems that have just been put in
place. The brain will continue to develop into the
50s, which is the final intellectual developmental
period for the brain.

Adolescence:

This period of development is a very difficult time for young people and their families because of the growth and transition from dependent to independent status. This stage of development is supposed to be rebellious! At this stage individuals consciously begin the "differentiation process" (knowing and understanding oneself) and also begin the completion of their social, emotional, physical, and sexual development. The emotional attachment at this level is primarily with peers, which is the prelude to making an emotional attachment with a partner as an adult.

Adolescence is an unstable time in an individual's development. In our culture, adolescents are launched into quasi-adulthood, with all the responsibilities and privileges that accompany it, but without being emotionally trained for the responsibilities that automatically accompany the adult privileges. The socialization process that usually starts in the family and continues into the school experiences has been noticeably ineffective over the last 20 years. The changes that have occurred in our society have been so dramatic and quick over the last 40 years that this pace may have contributed to the fact that our youth have a difficult time with social responsibility.

At around age 18 individuals begin to complete the biological adolescent phase and begin the process of finding their place within the larger frame of society. Their ability to take on more social reponsibility becomes apparent. It is an intense time for youth. Some theorists have stated that adolescence is also the optimal time for creativity because the adolescent is still able to imagine effortlessly outside traditional thought.

Emotional attachment now is becoming more complex because adolescents have experimented with peer attachment and now need to evolve emotionally before they are successful in taking on an adult life-time commitment, as expected in our society. They are still learning to connect with peers and bond emotionally, sexually, and socially with others.

Adolescents' sense of self is still fairly primitive and is heavily influenced by their peers. The transition from adolescent to adult is phenomenal in its development. Our culture is gradually eliminating childhood and we are creating little adults in spite of the knowledge that children are not adults. Unfortunately, we dress our children like adults, incorporating the sexual connotation, without the social responsibility that needs to accompany the behaviours. I believe this systematic elimination of childhood is creating a profound challenge for our youth.

Adulthood:

An individual's personality is not usually completely formulated until about 21-25, depending on the individual and their life experiences. The perception of herself at 19 will be dramatically different of herself after 25. Her needs will also reflect the dramatic differences in her self perception. There are tremendous social expectations at this stage of development, as our society relies totally on this group to support the entire society financially, socially, and emotionally, whether it is a small community on a south sea island or a continent.

Now, how does all of this impact communication? Communication starts with self. How do I communicate with me? What tools did I learn in my life experiences? What defense mechanisms are comfortable and effective? A toddler at a year old has already formally started the process. Psychologists believe a baby's request for breast milk, by making some stressful sounds, are the first attempts to communicate. The success and how that success is perceived by the baby/toddler becomes the foundation of the perception of confidence in communicating with others.

An example is when my husband and I had our first baby, we thought nothing of sleeping with the baby. Unfortunately by the time the baby was a year old, it was becoming a stressful situation. Neither one of us was sleeping properly and I believe, nor was my son. Well, I thought the natural response to all our discomfort was to put my son in his crib at night and not bring him to our bed when he cried. My ignorance was powerful and emotionally painful but very enlightening!

The first night I was not successful because his crying pushed all of my buttons about hurting his feelings. I believe that I was more devastated then he was. The second, third night, and even two weeks later I was no longer a happy camper, nor was my son. I could not let him cry. I became so tired that I was walking around like a zombie. Finally, I talked myself into being my notion of a "bad mother" and I was going to let him cry. It was a wonderful education. After the first 45 minutes, I began to really listen to his cry. It was not distressed but insulted. That first night was long but rewarding. He finally fell asleep after two and a half hours. He woke up his normal time the next morning, happy and energized, while I was hollow-eyed and dragging myself out of bed. What a surprise! I had been emotionally traumatized and he was back to normal.

It took four more nights of marathon crying before he realized that he was not going to sleep with us anymore. It was worth the emotional pain, because I learned something about myself. I had been more invested in supporting my notion of a good mother rather than being an effective mother who had a happy, independent child. The "good mother" was all about how I wanted to perceive myself. The "effective mother" was more realistic and in the process I gave my son the gift of independence, which is the building block of self-confidence. By self-soothing he gained the confidence to be alone and to enjoy it. His learning to self-soothe set the foundation for his learning self reliance and building self-confidence.

The process of differentiation that was mentioned earlier, starts with independence. A child needs to learn to be self-contained because she then learns to understand her feelings. It is that understanding that begins the process of knowing and understanding one's self. Babies, when they cry, learn to self-soothe; it is a critical step in learning to survive emotional trauma later in life. My son eventually learned to soothe himself when he realized that I was not coming to his rescue. If a child doesn't learn to self-soothe she will have a difficult time building self-trust, which translates into self-confidence.

What I learned in my childhood about communication I could stuff in a thimble. My family members were not skilled communicators and they were still *reacting* to emotional trauma. This created a dysfunctional family. I was not able to understand my disadvantage until I was an adult myself with my own family. Many families are not able to teach productive, meaningful, and fulfilling communication skills. It is unfortunate because this is the most effective and natural place to learn the skill of communicating thoughts, feelings, and ideas.

It is logical to make the assumption that we learn who we are by the perceptions of the people that are part of the attachment process we experience. It is only when we are adults that we can productively and effectively deal with who we are.

Abraham Mazlow, one of the great-grandfathers of psychoanalysis, claimed that we can only reach this level of development when we are physically, financially, emotionally, and socially secure in our worlds. He coined the term self-actualization. This refers to the need to know about one's self within the society in which one lives and to understand who one is, within this framework.

Self-actualization appears to be a luxury for most of us. If life is so challenging that I am spending most of my energy on surviving financially, then I won't have the energy to spend on self-understanding further than how it directly impacts my survival.

At approximately 35, human development literally stops and we begin the process of ageing. This fact supports Mazlow's theory, in that most people begin to assess their life existence, because they are now more than ever aware of how they are a small part of the world they live in. Before this, a young adult may still think she is immortal and that life is for her to experience with no thought to what part she plays in this world.

One of the biggest challenges we all face is articulating the unconscious lessons learned by reading body language and learning the hidden rules and messages that our families teach us. It is so engrained in our communication styles and skills that it presents a real challenge many times to understand why we think what we think as our perception of our world changes. The adult who has now achieved autonomy and has begun the process of emotional self-awareness is able to view herself as only a small element in the scheme of things in her world.

For example when my son was old enough to open the fridge door I became agitated. My first inclination was to stop him. I still unconsciously believed that children didn't have the right to look or take food from the fridge. What stopped me from acting on my inclination was the absurdity of the notion. What was my son going to do? Was he going to get hurt? Was there something in the fridge that could hurt him? There was really no safety issue here. But my family of origin had a rule that children didn't have access to the fridge. So the task was to teach my son about how the fridge kept things cold and not to leave the door open too long. When he couldn't reach something he wanted, he needed to learn to ask for help.

I was reprogramming my paradigm of family rules. I came up against this over and over again and was forced to really look at why the rule existed and if it had a basis in safety. In the reprogramming I was forced to realize just how dysfunctional my notion of childhood expectations were. It was a valuable lesson in parenting for me.

Couplehood another milestone in adult development naturally stimulates and continues the self-awareness process. The more self-aware I am the more I can share who I am with my partner. In the marital and family therapy theories, the reason that couplehood provides the best environment for self-awareness is because couples naturally evolve together to survive. The conflicts and tensions that are a natural source of energy provide the stimulation for a couple to change. This stimulation is the reason why the couple needs to do the personal work to better understand themselves and the relationship that is constantly evolving.

When one partner perceives a change in her world it impacts the other partner. This natural friction that occurs is necessary to assist the evolution of self that would reflect the evolution of the couplehood.

A personal example was when I decided to go back to school to continue my education in another field,once my children had started school full time. I had been in administration before I gave up my employment to become a stay-home parent. It was natural for my husband to think that I would return to the commercial world and take up where I left off. I wasn't emotionally in that place. Instead, I wanted to attend university and become a special educator. My husband was shocked and emotionally traumatized because my decision impacted our family finances and our parental roles. By my husband's adjusting and aborbing the trauma of change he was able to also change his perception of himself. His role of breadwinner was changed, his role of parent changed, since he needed to pick up the slack when I was no longer always available for the children.

This same experience occurred for me, too. I needed to revisit my priorities. Keeping the kitchen floor spotless was no longer practical. Sharing my kitchen was now a necessity. Living in a home that was more lived-in became a reality through survival.

These life situations provide the couplehood with challenges that enrich the couplehood and the partners working together.

Types of Depression

Couplehood with all of its inherent developmental changes and challenges, may sometimes be more challenging because one partner suffers from depression.

This chapter is a brief overview of depressions. There are two types of major depression. One is psychological and the other is physiological. In this chapter I will try to help you understand what depression is and whether or not you will need professional help so that it does not impact your couplehood negatively.

Chemical imbalances are physiological in nature and are usually believed to be inherited through genes. A chemical imbalance that causes depression usually needs medical treatment. The physiologically depressed person will not be able to come out of the depression without professional and medical intervention. It can be very debilitating emotionally because the person may feel that her body is out of control. This lack of control is more than scary and help is essential for this depressed person to feel emotionally and physically safe.

Also, the implications of mental illness set this type of depression apart from psychological depression. It is a very difficult notion to accept when suffering from a chemical imbalance. There are so many ideas at play. Most times the chemical imbalances are genetic. If a person should suffer a brain injury this may trigger the imbalance, but most times the physiological depression is commonly considered genetic, therefore a life sentence that was never fairly negotiated. This fact alone is a form of emotional trauma.

Treatment for chemical imbalances will never be just an anti-depressant. It usually includes more than one drug to counter the condition. A medical

assessment from a psychiatrist is strongly recommended and the family physician will need
to consult with a psychiatrist for effective treatment. People who suffer from chemical imbalances are courageous and tenacious in their need
to survive. They need to be honoured.

Counselling is recommended and it may be for
periods at a time for most of the person's adult
life. The trauma of having a chemical imbalance
is significant and because it is an imbalance, the
trauma is never really gone. So each episode or
depressive state experienced needs to be assisted
with clinical counselling and medical monitoring.

Psychological Depression is usually caused by
emotional trauma. This type of depression is usually experienced after an emotionally traumatic
event. But sometimes the psychological depression may be experienced for very long periods
of time. If the environment is toxic for the individual the depression will last as long as the
toxicity is present.

Treatment may sometimes include medical intervention with anti-depressants prescribed by a
family physician. Clinical counselling is usually

needed as well to help the individual to understand how to absorb the emotional trauma without being traumatized again.

For the person suffering from depression her world is not a happy place. The ability to feel joy is almost non-existent. The body's response to depression is exhausting. The energy needed to just get through the day can be traumatic. A person suffering from depression needs to deal with the lack of joy and get treatment for the condition. She needs to honour both her vulnerability and her strength to get through this traumatic experience. The need to be empowered is essential in dealing with depression.

Therefore couplehood is even more of a challenge for both the depressed and the non-depressed partner. The conservative estimate is that about 30% of couples will include a depressed partner. Both partners will need to be gentle with themselves in learning to deal and live with depression.

Differentiating

The term differentiating is a psychological idea that means a form of emotional independence of others and a separation of feeling from thought. I believe that this concept is the driving force that dictates success for couplehood. This is another paradox! This independence implies that I would not be impacted or influenced unduly by another's feelings and thoughts.

Realistically I would say that this is impossible. To be independent of others for me has a rather different tone. When confronted with a conflicting value or new idea, I need to run through my repertoire of the core values that I am consciously aware of. My partner presenting the value or new idea plays a major role in my ability to understand and accept the new idea because of the intimacy between the two of us. To accept a new idea from my partner there needs to be a level of trust that comes from our intimacy. This can be a double-edged sword. I need to trust myself first, and then I am able to trust my partner.

An example was that when my husband and I were building our log house, we encountered a lot of conflicts in choosing materials and appliances. We were both coming at it from different angles. It became a lot easier and more comfortable to give each other permission to "win" the conflict if it was really a strong personal choice. I wanted carpet laid in the living room but not on the whole floor in the living room. I wanted carpet only laid where the TV central area was. Once it was laid, against my husband's better judgement and the carpet layer, both agreed that it was rather attractive and it had distinct advantages.

The dynamics that were in play were, that my husband and I needed to separate our feelings and our thoughts. It was not about 'you are not listening to me,' ' or you are not giving me a fair chance to honour my ideas,' but rather the thoughts were dominating the interaction because it was more about new ideas that were not conservative or widely accepted. It was not about my feeling judged, but rather challenged instead to convince others that my idea had merit.

The communication between my husband and me was playful but forceful. He realized that I was really convinced that this idea was important to try because I was able to give him valid reasons for wanting the partial carpet laid. When I felt challenged, I was not taking the lack of acceptance of my new idea personally because I understood that it was not a common practice. Instead, I took the challenge and tried very hard to convince my husband of the financial, practical, and ascetic advantages of laying carpet only in the TV area.

The difficult task of each individual is to assess the situation and then try not to take it personally. This is easier said than done in couplehood because of the intimacy. The notion of differentiation implies that the more I am intimate with myself, the more I can be intimate with my partner. This intimacy is based on self-awareness. The ability to not take my partner's feelings and thoughts personally becomes a real challenge in self-awareness. The **3-step model of self-communication** is constantly in play to avoid a possible chance that I am taking it personally.

When a situation has become embarrassing because I have made a misjudgement, it is almost instinctive for people intimate with me to feel judged by association. It takes a tremendous effort to think through the situation and not feel judged. How many times have we felt embarrassed by what our children have said or done in pure innocence? It becomes even more intense when it is our partner.

My husband and daughter always find an opportunity to tell the story of me asking the restaurant server for a bag to take home for my pigs the food I wasn't able to finish. They were more offended than the server. My daughter jumped to my rescue because she was trying to help me save face, or so she thought. I was not embarassed nor was the server. My daughter explained that we had a hobby farm and yes, there really were pigs!

The essential skills that were discussed in *Es-*

sential Skills (p. 21) compliment this form of intimacy or self-awareness. When couples talk *with* each other rather than *at* each other, they are practising the separation of feelings from thoughts. The **3-step model of self-communication** becomes a paramount tool in separating feelings from thoughts.

The essential skill of *discussing personal issues* that expose vulnerabilities implies a sense of confidence in self and the partner who is witnessing the vulnerable display. When I realize that my husband is not responsible for my happiness, that only I can be, then I understand the power in being vulnerable with my partner. When I understand that I am not responsible for my husband's happiness, that only he can be, then I realize that I cannot take personally the conflicts that will naturally come up in an intimate relationship. Couplehood is always dynamic, with conflicts to provide a forum for building self-awareness, self-confidence, and trust.

Couples who *avoid and accept old issues of resolved conflict* are honouring themselves in this essential skill. They have separated their thoughts from their feelings and are able to move on without losing trust in themselves or their partner. The process of resolution becomes a tool in building the self-awareness and the intimate awareness of their partner.

Paraphrasing an important essential skill is critical in truly understanding the importance of my feelings or thoughts. It translates into understanding and accepting my husband's feelings and thoughts because they are separate from mine and so it is important I understand them in order to accept them. If my husband's feelings are hurt from something I said, it does not mean that my feelings are hurt, too. This idea is extremely simple but it becomes very complicated in couplehood communication. I feel the pain that my husband feels but I need to know that it is my empathy and not my personal feelings that are being felt. The evaluation of the hurt feelings is based upon my intent. If I am honouring my feelings my intent is respectful, even though the content of the message maybe painful.

The more *sensitive* I am to my own feelings and thoughts, the more *sensitive* I will need to be to my partner's feelings and thoughts. My awareness is an invaluable essential skill. This awareness of my partner's feelings and thoughts builds tremendous trust and acceptance. This sensitivity is usually a gradual development that comes with resolving conflicts. The need to separate feelings from thoughts is practised repeatedly in order to become fluent and skilled in being sensitive to my feelings and my partner's feelings as two different entities.

When I think that an emotional issue has been resolved it never fails to crop back up without warning and bite me in the nose. The ability to field that emotional issue is important in honouring my *openness to revisiting an emotional area* that needs to be worked through because I was not emotionally ready before when the issue first came up. I need for my partner to be aware of how this emotional issue has impacted me again. I help him to learn about my vulnerability to this emotional issue by sharing my feelings and thoughts with him. I do not need for him to take my vulnerability personally; I am the only one who can look after me. I want his empathy only. This process is another essential skill.

Being sensitive to my partner's feelings usually is determined by my skill in *reading his body language*. I am receptive to changes in his body language and with experience I recognize vital and sometimes subtle changes that indicate what is happening emotionally for him. It helps that my partner trusts me to not hide his feelings from me but allows me to witness and share them with him. He can only do that if he is self-confident enough which comes from his self-awareness.

Feeling accepted by my partner is absolutely, positively necessary and I believe the most difficult and essential skill. By working at becoming skilled in the essential skills I am committing myself to accepting all of me and by so doing, am also committing to accepting all of my partner.

Couplehood may be a dramatic and brilliantly coloured quilt, or it may be quiet with a complex pattern. Couplehood still functions as a wonderful theatre for self-awareness, which builds self-confidence. The constant changes and demands made by an evolving couplehood can be invaluable in learning about myself. The only constant in couplehood is change. Change of life circumstances, change of emotional growth, which is a constant evolution of self, are ideally and naturally supported by the couplehood.

I believe today that couplehood is more rewarding but also more challenging. Social roles have changed or become obsolete. Social environments have become more demanding and isolated because of economics. Social expectations have become unclear and sometimes contradictory. Couples need to honour these challenges and be gentle with themselves in their efforts to make a rewarding and complimentary long-term union that thrives on risk-taking.

Glossary

Attachment: a psychological term referring to the emotional bonding that needs to occur between the caregivers and the newborn.

Core value: is a personality trait that is inherent and supports a life behaviour value. An example would be a person who is able to stay in control during a crisis but falls apart after the crisis. This is not consciously done but inherent in the makeup of the individual.

Critical Period: a period of development where the neurological stimulation needs to occur to create the necessary development because if it should not, the opportunity will not occur again.

Depression: a state of mind that impacts detrimentally a person's sense of self and his/her behaviours.

Differentiation: a psychological term used by marital and family theorists, that describes the process of self-awarenss.

Dirty fighting: unskilled behaviours that are disrespectful in nature but are used to protect a sense of self.

Disassociation: is a behaviour where the individual emotionally disconnects from the ocurring situation.

Double standards: criticising another for the same behaviour that is employed by the individual who is criticizing another.

Empathy: the ability to truly understand another's feelings through personally having experienced the feeling.

Empowering: is when the individual is consciously aware of how s/he is in control of his/her sense of self. Feelings are not fearful but educational, and behaviours honour the notion of feeling in control of self when a situation is occurring.

Fair fighting: skilled behaviours that are respectful and assertive in nature.

Imagination: the ability to use all sense outside the realm of physical reality.

Mores: specific hidden or un-written rules of conduct that are understood and expected by members of a specific culture.

Osmosis: the learning about our world at a profoundly unconscious level.

Paradigm: an unconsious understanding that is reflected in conscious behaviour.

Paraphrasing: a skill where an individual re-peats the message given back to the individual who has given the message, using the receiver's own words and perception.

Patronization: to condescend another

Personality: the combination of character traits that makes one person unique.

Reacting: to behave without thinking through the behaviour.

Readiness: used in a psychological sense where the emotional and physical elements of a person are able to withstand an emotional trauma.

Responding: to behave after thinking through

the situation and making a decision about the behaviour of choice in response to the situation.

Self-Soothe: a skills that creates a feeling of safety that needs to be learned in order to begin a healthy foundation for future autonomy as an adult.

Socialization: the process by which an individual learns social behaviours, attitudes, and values held by the specific social group.

Sympathy: to share the painful feeling but not to have an innate understanding from experience.

Temperament: the natural inclination or mode of emotional response that characterizes an individual.

Trauma: emotional shock that has lasting effects on the person traumatized. The degree of trauma is unique to each individual and is determined by the perception of the degree of emotional shock.

Bibliography

Bowlby, John. A Secure Base: Parent-Child Attachment and Healthy Human Development. Basic Books. 1988.

Caplan, Theresa & Frank. The Early Childhood Years: The 2 to 6 Year Old. Bantam Books. 1984.

Curran, Dolores. Traits of a Healthy Family. Ballantine Books. 1983.

Dass, Ram & Gorman, Paul. How Can I Help?. Alfred A, Knopf. 1985.

Fast, Julius. Creative Coping: A Guide to Positive Living. William Morrow & Co. Inc. 1976.

Frankl, Victor. E. Man's Search for Meaning. First Pocket Books, 1983.

Fromm, Erich. The Art of Loving. Pernnial Library. 1956.

Galinsky, Ellen. <u>The Six Stages of Parenthood</u>. Addison-Wesley Publishing Co. 1987.

Gotman, John. <u>Why Marriages Succeed or Fail: and How You Can Make Yours Last</u>. Fireside Book. 1994.

Hall, Edward. T. <u>The Silent Language</u>. Double-day Anchor Book. 1973.

Harris, Thomas. A. <u>I'm OK – You're OK</u>. Avon Books. 1967.

Healy, Jane. M. <u>Your Child's Growing Mind</u>. Doubleday. 1987.

Kaplan, Louise. J. <u>Oneness and Separateness</u>. A Touchstone Book. 1978.

Miller, Sherod. Miller, Phyllis. Nunnally, Elam. W. Wackman, Daniel. B. <u>Talking and Listening Together</u>. Interpersonal Communication Program Inc. 1991.

Morris, Desmond. <u>Intimate Behaviour</u>. Random House. 1971.

Morris, Desmond. <u>The Naked Ape: A Zoologist's Study of the Human Animal</u>. Johnathan Cape. 1967.

Napier, Augustus. Y. & Whitaker, Carl. <u>The Family Crucible: The Intense Experience of Family Therapy. 1978</u>.

Nicols, Michael. P. & Schwartz, Richard. C. <u>Family Therapy: Concepts and Methods</u>. Allyn and Bacon. 4th edition. 1998.

Nicols, William. C. <u>Treating People in Families</u>. The Guilford Press. 1996.

Scarf, Maggie. <u>Intimate Partners: Patterns in Love and Marriage</u>. Ballantine Publishing Group. 1987.

Scarf, Maggie. <u>Intimate Worlds: How Families Thrive and Why They Fail</u>. Ballantine Publishing Group. 1995.

Scarf, Maggie. <u>Unfinished Business: Pressure Point in the Lives of Women</u>. Ballantine Publishing Group. 1985.

Schnarch, David. Constructing the Sexual Crucible: An Integration of Sexual and Marital Therapy. W.W.Norton & Co. 1991.

Schnarch, David. Passionate Marriage. Henry Holt & Co. 1998.

Sharf, Richard. S. Theories of Psychotherapy and Counseling. Brooks / Cole Publishing Co. 1996.

Smith-Rohberg, Duncan. *Interactions Between Mental States, Physiology, and Immunity.* The Harvard Brain. Vol 7,[Spring 2000]

Wilbur, Ken. Engler, Jack. & Brown, Daniel. P. Transformations of Consciousness. Shambhala Publications Inc. 1986.

Williamson, Donald. S. The Intimacy Paradox. The Guilford Press. 1991.

Notes: